Woman Without Umbrella

Also by Victoria Redel

Poetry:

Swoon
Already the World

Fiction:

Where the Road Bottoms Out
Loverboy
The Border of Truth

Woman Without Umbrella

Victoria Redel

FOUR WAY BOOKS
TRIBECA

Please direct all inquiries to:
Editorial Office
Four Way Books
POB 535, Village Station
New York, NY 10014
www.fourwaybooks.com

Library of Congress Cataloging-in-Publication Data

Redel, Victoria.
 [Poems. Selections]
 Woman without umbrella / Victoria Redel.
   pages cm
 ISBN 978-1-935536-24-6 (pbk.)
 I. Title.
 PS3568.E3443W66 2012
 811'.54--dc23

                         2012002008

This book is manufactured in the United States of America
and printed on acid-free paper.

Four Way Books is a not-for-profit literary press. We are grateful for the assistance
we receive from individual donors, public arts agencies, and private foundations.

State of the Arts

NYSCA

This publication is made possible with public funds
from the New York State Council on the Arts, a state agency.

[clmp]   We are a proud member
             of the Council of Literary Magazines and Presses.

Distributed by University Press of New England
One Court Street, Lebanon, NH 03766

For Nancy Rockland-Miller—brave, resilient, luminous friend.
And for my sister, Jessica.

Contents

&

&

THE WAY IT BEGAN

Chapter 1

They went, not in the day, but then in the dark with no shoes on their feet, the road pokey with broke-up shell.

And the boy to the girl, Let's be quick.
I can't, said the girl. My feet are girly.

The boy to the girl, That'll change, and held back a branch, thought she'd passed but heard the snap and then the girl, Can't you even try being nice?

Chapter 2

By day, by the river, they kept to scrub, hid among boulders, slept with their shoulders cool against granite.

Just wind, he said, wind heard in the night, whushed through fir trunks. By morning the woods quiet, not a limb cracked on the path.

Chapter 3

He was afraid of kind words in the dark.

Chapter 4

She was afraid of finding a heart safety-pinned inside her jacket.

Chapter 5

Berries in the brush, tart against tongues, the boy's lips stained, Like a girl, the girl said.
The boy to the girl, You'd like that.
The girl laughed and said, I guess we'll find out.

Chapter 6

Was she afraid she'd grow wings?

Chapter 7

Was he worried she'd always sleep next to him?

Chapter 8

They came to a town, kept to its limit. Lights on in houses and then lights off.

The boy to the girl, Do you miss much of it?
Not what I thought I'd miss, said the girl.

Chapter 9

The boy woke scared and woke the girl.
Shoes and toast, said the girl to calm the boy.
And the boy to the girl, Toast and milk.

Then the girl, Milk and toast and shoes and soap.
And the boy to the girl, We better stop this and go to sleep.

Chapter 10

Rain, then not.
Dry ground, dry riverbed, knotty bramble and burr stuck so they picked at each other,

Like animals, said the boy combing fingers through her hair.
Good ones, said the girl licking salt from his arm.

Chapter 11

The girl to the boy, Will it always be this way?

Chapter 12

The boy to the girl, Can you even remember the way it began?

&

THE END

At the end of the marriage they lay down on their big, exhausted bed.
It was crowded with all the men and women they had ever loved.

Of course their fathers and mothers were there and a boy in uniform
she'd kissed on a stairwell. His first wife spooned her first husband.

Ridiculous Affair held hands with Stupendous Infatuation.
There was a racket of dreaming and, though both were tired

from the difficult end and in need of sleep, neither could sleep,
so they began telling each other the long, good story of their love.

She was wearing the red dress. The white boat hitched to the wood dock
filled with rainwater. The swans were again teaching the young to fly.

The story went out to nice dinners, took summer holidays, and by the time
they were done, the old loves rolled over in a jumble on the floor,

and, because this is what they knew to do well with one another,
they made love, and then without thinking it was the last time, said,

I love you, and fell asleep under the heavy, blue coverlet.

SAY IT

The roof collapses. The door shuts with the key inside.
It starts to rain and there's no party tent. The pills run out.

She still can't sleep. His heart can't say yes.
Perhaps they wake, years later, different zones, different beds.

She thinks of a joke he once told. He thinks
how she shook her head and words tangled in his mouth.

Outside, rivers thrash the banks. There's fighting
North. Migrations East with nothing on their backs.

Encampments along the border, metal shacks bulldozed
against the full-on glare. She reads about shortages.

There are recommendations. What each needs to give up.
And she thinks, I can't. Won't. Don't want to. Will.

METRO DINER

Alexi, my breakfast waiter, says it's about time he teaches me
how to get by in Greece. *S'agapo poli*, he says to me. You'll say it,

he says, maybe the third time with a Greek man.
Where am I? Who's the Greek? I say. What third time?

Alexi says, Please, just practice.
S'agapo poli, I say with each refill of coffee. *S'agapo poli*,

when he takes my finished platter of egg whites, potatoes and toast.
That's not quite right, he says, or, Slower, or, Again.

Then, You're ready, he says. Now you will go to Greece.
I say it one last time, stand from the booth, and go out onto 100th

and Broadway where a father and his daughter pass holding hands.
In his other hand swings a pink Hello Kitty backpack.

Guys unload crates from double-parked produce trucks.
The street cleaning machine sweeps uptown.

A man and woman stop to kiss before going off into separate days.
Only ever you, she calls without looking back.

In stories the Genie gives three wishes. It's a mystical number,
third chain in the link, connected to the second, original from the first.

Three fates, three graces, Plato's thirds. My sons last night
at dinner, high-fiving forks, calling, Three strikes, you're out!

11

Now, on 97th, a Bengali shopkeeper shutters open his metal newsstand.
In a salon window, a woman's head tented in highlight foils.

Walking by Gourmet Garage, smoky retsina, olives by the barrel,
savory offerings for a Hellenic picnic—each, a postcard to the future

where I show-up, wearing something ropy, Ionic, draped for the Divine.

CIRCE

She thinks she should apologize
that she still loves a man's body this much,

the line of hair, now mown with gray,
wandering thin and messy down

the sloped stomach, and his stomach,
even there, just under where he's thickened,

the hard ridge and jag of muscle,
an old athlete story he's telling

when he pulls onto those blown out
knees, wrestling her up against his hips

which work their game though sometimes
a new, slower, easier game she didn't know

to ask for back then, though back then,
he reminds her now with a quickening,

worked exactly right too, so when
she yanks close, grabbing the softened,

thinned neck skin, she looks—
once she took them only for their turned,

lost, cloven surprise—but now
this slight hanging slump of cheek

and the blueish pouch rimmed under
those eyes—the effort across this man's face

as he yields—there, as he was,
always, finally, that bright absolute.

WOLF

Bad, bad, he says, when what he means is good,
how it was to see the girl,

just a red smell to him then,
a poor dress caught in the wind.

She was the wrong door, the blind stairwell.
He was who he had always been.

Bad, bad, he says, when what he needs to say
is how they kept to the woods, the day a twist

and the girl gone close to that far away.
If he could be the street, the floor,

a rug of mothy wool he would beg her to walk
back and forth on till she shred a worn path.

Knock knock, he says, when what he means is come in.
Knock, he says, when what he means is he knows who's there.

Are you listening? If you are, save me from this story.

WOMAN WITHOUT UMBRELLA, TAROT

It went like this: disaster, disaster, ridiculously bad disaster,

until she somehow woke into a calm easy every day

that her friends tried, to no avail, to convince her might actually be love.

WOMAN WITHOUT UMBRELLA, UNSEASONABLE

All month her city sweats and sticks,
women and men stripped down to a snarl, *it's too fucking hot.*

These are steamy low-key days, south of the border,
hot-to-the-touch afternoons,

burning cement walls built for pressing him up against.

SUDDENLY

A month after turning forty-five, every last egg in her body
is a Rockette doing the can-can. Use me use me use me, they cry.
I'll be the easy child, the I-won't-wake-you-up-in-the-night child.

Now every city block boasts the popular miracle—

Keep away, she says to civilized men who stop at crosswalks.
Do you see this glittered fertility, this fishnet stocking hunger?

The possible calls and the body lunges—rapacious—for what?—Every
last urgency to be the body?

WOMAN WITHOUT UMBRELLA

Thus she waited at the corner
for the light to change.

Indeed sometimes she wanted to sneak
back and have another look.

Then she was afraid,
actually, it was a lot simpler than she'd let on.

Therefore and then, indeed, and somewhat and thus.

Nevertheless there were accidents
and other misfortunes.

AND GRACE, FRIDAY

Then I read a story by a friend and I cried. It would just keep happening—this friend dead. That friend sick. Already so many impossible—but such sweet—loves.

Maybe this was it—finito, caput. No more loves, possible or impossible.

And in the middle—ah, rotten, elaborate self-pity!—my son's, Come on, Mom, why always last minute? (If his medical, trip, and emergency forms weren't in this day then that would be that.)

So I grumbled across the Park to his school, then rode the 6 to Union Square's Green market—immediately needing every heirloom tomato, wanting fresh sausage and whole chickens who'd led happy lives on farms and bunches of pink cosmos and white dahlias so there were too many non-biodegradable bags to carry the six blocks to the doctor's where she confirmed, That's really something, examining my face.

Then because I'd been assured life with a prescription and a cream, I treated myself to a cab.

The driver put my bags in the trunk saying, I'll tie these up like I do my wife's, so everything's safe.

His cab turned onto the West Side Highway. It's a lovely day, he said. I looked around and now the day looked okay. We arrived at my street. Thanks for letting me drive you, he said handing over my bags. No, thank you, I said. And he said, Please, the thanks are all mine.

I shut up to give him the last word.

In the apartment my son and his friends were undoing their collective intelligence with video games. Hey, Mom, he said. And the other boys, Amadi, Kareem, Sam, and James said, Hey, Mom.

I said, Anyone hungry? And they—pretty much at once—said, Me.

EASY LIVING

My friend made it seem easy to die,
so busy with everyday business,

taking his step-boy for he-men pizza
after band practice and waking his wife

so they'd have another round
of eagle-feathered love before her shift.

Then, mornings, he came at it again,
vitamins, good food, army pushups,

before he sat at his desk howling
his story which had many pages

of muscle and heart. Forgive him
if the end felt abrupt. If he forgot to tell us

what came next. Didn't get it
all done. Didn't have time to die before dying.

FIRST

Most days we were fools
for the French thing,

went at it all twirl
and twirl. Or took

our good time, breaks
to catnap our tongues.

Wherever you are, driving
whichever back road

of suburban middle-age,
whatever courage

brings you through
to whomever you love,

there it is again,
the old frontier.

Slow down, good man.
Open the window, good woman.

LATER STILL, THEN

What if I told the husband everything.

How I leaned against a shoulder on the raft. Later, still. Or years earlier. And then.

About the island, only the island.

What if the husband told me all that he could tell me.

How, right now, for instance, at these years' distance, he hears an acute, tender longing and wants to shout.

WOMAN WITHOUT UMBRELLA

Her affection,

like light,
zig-zagged over the lake.

Every one of the friends said, It's okay, are you still there?

She'd had the thought before,
then lost it.

Then or before that?

The bird out of one tree, landing in the next.

They said they could see what she'd sort of meant.
As if nothing had happened.

She said, Are you sure you know what you're doing?
She swore she didn't know how it had turned to that.

The dark came on with orange in the clouds.
Swallows feeding over the lake.

No one had anything left to say.

If she hadn't said it before, or enough, she was sorry.

AT THE BUSY INTERSECTION

When I saw the man tuck the boy
under his arm like a chicken
or a football, it made me
remember how after one week
of pre-season my youngest declared
his body was all wrong,
insufficient to take down boys
he needed taken down. Our home
became a chapel to muscle—
bench presses, free-weights, protein
powders, capsules of creatine.

It made me miss my mother.
The way in winter, she'd say,
Don't breathe, when we walked from
the house to the blue Chevrolet.
She was always begging a doctor
to give us penicillin shots,
something I understand when
my eldest calls from the midwest,
Don't worry, Mom, but I'm very sick.

I can't say I'm worried exactly
about the boy under the man's arm
but I'm not unworried either.
If it were up to me,
the man would set the boy down
and they'd hold hands
to cross the dangerous street.

If it were up to me—I hear
my mother cluck. And the rest
of them, too, who watch our lives
like sitcom, like a sports match,
side-splitting amusement for
the honking, neighing, barnyard dead.

UPGRADE

I don't want a refund to say it didn't fit, never worked, or worked at first,
then in fits and starts, the switches useless, gears stripped. No, I don't want

Customer Service, a Claims Department, complaint letters, an exchange
or credit toward the latest model, an upgrade or Lifetime Parts Replacement.

Even now, broken, chipped, in pieces, pieces lost, worn out, the original
gone—there are times, still, it comes back to me whole and I am amazed

by what is beyond fragile, by how elaborately and generously, wrecked
and beyond repair, we made use of our hearts all those years. And then.

BOTTOM LINE

As when my father goes back under
and the doctor comes out to tell us he's put a window in my father's heart.

At last! The inscrutable years are over. I'll look right in
before the glass gets smudged, before he has a chance to buy drapes or
      slatted blinds.

It will be a picture window; I'll be a peeping tom.
Imagine the balcony of secrets, the longings: our future a window box of
      heart-to-hearts.

Then he's awake, calling for morphine,
his pain greater than from the first surgery.

On the next rounds the doctor clarifies:
the window's really more like a gutter so built-up fluids can drain.

And I remember my father on a ladder
pulling down leaves and rot, each year saying, Do I need this kind of
      trouble?

Saying, A new roof? You think I'm made of money?
Draw the shades. Let him rest. Let me sit beside my father in the dark.

HIS EXCUSE

He told her the story of his grandfather's donkey. He said, This donkey was known as a good donkey, maybe the best donkey in the village. My grandfather loved the donkey. Maybe more than his sons. Definitely more than his wife. The donkey got past the fence—once, twice—and, finally, the neighbor came to my grandfather saying, Your donkey has been in my garden. Can't you keep your donkey where it belongs? the neighbor said to my grandfather. My grandfather said, Yes. No Problem. I will keep my donkey out of your garden. And he took his gun and shot his donkey in the head.

UNDER THE RADAR

As if I admit it aloud, even once—the gods' bitch slap of eternal suffering.

Instead, before only a raft of cloud and the V of green hills that faces
        the ocean,
let me quietly come to where you read in the slatted chair.

I touch your hair. You do not look up. Not even the slyest smile, partner
        in this crime.
Which means you understand our severity exactly.

ALMOST FIFTY

PE

Not wanting, he insists, but if, he says,
if somehow it happened, how he imagines

she'd frisk back onto the bed to tell him,
light from the skylight shifting

through the room, across her face,
and then, despite everything—

her children, his children, the too
many hours already spent

at too many jobs—how they couldn't
help wanting the impossible—swaddled

and delivered into late middle age—
to grow between them—brilliant bones,

first steps, lost barrettes and mitts,
that sparkling, exhausting amazement.

Which is why, talking in bed till noon,
they're undone by each inconceivable loss.

TODAY, WE'RE THIS WORLD'S DARLING

All the trees on Broadway thrill white petals,
daffodils gather in bouquets to fling
themselves at us like schoolgirls. Shopkeepers lean
from doors, tip hats, toss candy and fish.
Sidewalks sparkle up to catch our eye.
Holy moly, even the incorrigible past has arrived
pledging it will finally learn goodness and mercy.

Don't look up. Don't wave back or wink.
Hurry off the avenue and bolt the door.
By tomorrow, snickering—show-off, fake—
they'll croon for Lindsey, or Nick's black eye.
The publicist of someone's rehabbed heart rumors
maples will turn gold for his comeback.

Ovid can tell you, give it fifteen minutes
and if you're lucky, you're banished to an island.
Or like Poe, your obit, written by the enemy
Griswald, declares in print, *Few will grieve.*
There's Bessie Smith in her unmarked grave.

Let biographers flock to the clever and pretty,
declare us old, drab, utterly last season.
And when they're gone, chasing the next fabulous
story, say again just one of the things
I can't repeat here. Those gorgeous, scandalous,
tender words you say to me each morning
that would make them quiver, that would change their lives.

AND THEN

What if, darling, tonight we tell only the best stories
we have of other loves. Not just nights of pleasure

but the way he laughed from the back of his throat,
the truthful thing she said that made you cry.

What about that spring wind. And when there was a bicycle,
a downpour, and someone had or didn't have a poncho.

Someone said the very thing you longed to hear.
You told a secret and were safe. She had a fever. He lost a father.

There were good meals. To think of those fine shoes
we scuffed about in thinking we were royalty.

And remember that plastic tiara and the clumsy pavane.
Remember what you wished. And how he wished, too.

Look at us now as we drink coffee, talk about the day's particulars
and possibilities. Morning light folds across the dark wood table.

Could we bear to look at one another knowing
how full the heart has already been. How we come

to one another not just thankful refugees from sorrow
but wild too, with easy days of mismatched socks.

This morning we think we couldn't be happier.
That's courage. We've thought it before.

&

KISSING

The first surprise of your mouth and mine.

On streets, on staircases, in bathrooms, in the backs of cabs, in a field, against that wall and that wall and that wall, down on the floor, my hair caught in it, in hotel beds, in a borrowed bed, and in the same bed night after night after year after night, through an open window, under pines, under water, on a raft, in rain, salty with ocean, a peck at the door, a have a good day.

Our mouths, prepositional.

Eyes open, eyes closed, your face in transport.

Combustible.

At the sink, doing dishes and suddenly you are turning me saying, "Give me your mouth," and I am giving you my mouth.

Coming up out of it, stunned.

Like there is another room inside and then another room inside.

Strawberries, sourness of coffee, a slight fizzy sweetness or the clean grass taste as only you taste.

Your face so close to mine.

A fluency, accented, each vowel and consonant exactly formed.

Sudden native speakers.

Mornings, just wakened, still slow and thick and dreaming, turning away from your reach.

Like something windy, like good weather. In winter, our mouths the warmest place in the city.

Kissing like nobody's business.

A lower lip flicked by teeth, pulling back just a little to breathe together.

And, then, all twitch and pull and ache.

Snuck, stolen, last, first, unbidden, forbidden, sloppy, delicious, French, farewell, slippery, criminal.

A private syntax.

Pun and slang, slip of tongue, intentional.

Could I have known on the Harwood building stairwell with my first, fast, dry, twelve-year-old kiss, that I'd become a woman who'd drive across state lines for the moment just before the kiss begins.

"What I miss is the make out. That's what I'd go for if I had a night on the lam," the married woman says, looking at a couple who have rolled off their picnic blanket.

One of us might say, "Only this," and then it's the first night all over again, tumble and wrestle, every mystical, dirty, delicious thing two mouths manage.

"Kiss me goodbye," you say, and on a street among strangers in floppy hats and winter coats, we slip into one another to say last apologies and promises.

In a bank line or sitting at a dinner table with friends, I touch my mouth.

I am drifting or you are drifting and one pressed against the other whispers, Goodnight.

The last one, the day's punctuation.

&

HOLY

Then I went to a party and danced like no tomorrow,
shaking and grooving, my arms in praise, my hips down to it,

busting out moves like I was rocking avenues past
Chelsea's techno clubs and trumped up Hell's Kitchen

through Harlem's newest renaissance to 167th and Fort Washington
where—intubated, on drips—she slept a monitored sleep,

beep beep beep beep, nurses in and out to put a line, take blood
and her broken and sewed chest—up down, up down—

with the ventilator's suck and whoosh that forced Saturday night into
Easter Sunday and we were, oldest friend, delivered unto another day.

GORGEOUS PRESENT

Just this instant Mr. Minard drove to our elementary school
with a life-sized cut-out of a lady in the front seat of his Impala

and I'm certain something beautiful whisked by unnoticed.

Gorgeous Present, sometimes, I confess, I'm hardly here, so busy
chasing the scrawny tail of my narratives in playground circles,

bouncing four-square and playing freeze tag back through hallways,

past Mr. S who push-broomed fallen pilgrims, torn snowflakes,
and paperclips from one end of the building to the other, where,

mixed with Bazooka wads, a mitten, the constant crumpled Kleenex,
     our day sorted.

Now I'm inside the music room winking at Charity Bailey,
as she gathers orderly circles of her white children to bend and jump

and sing, *Gonna-jump-down-turn-around-pick-a-bale-a-cotton.*

Over and over we learn the future is now—though then was so new
and shiny, corridors that led to cursive and multiplication's possibility,

even glass hallways where birds crashed—stunned, broken—dropped

to the gravel. We took those deaths in stride. Everything ahead
or faraway back in the heroic, mythic land Mrs. Brennan shows

when she holds open a library book, enchanting, *Once upon a time.*

Turn a page and see late afternoons where Mr. S. crouches
to splint a starling's leg or sweep the dead

so that each morning the allegiance we pledge is new.

It is so noisy in me, these uncompleted tales.

Then Mr. Minard drives his lady home.
See the frozen single-serving he bakes then eats

while she waits stiffly in the scented car.

BACK

Over my dead body, our mother used to say.

As if that would stop us from jumping in puddles.

Or into the back of fast cars. As if—when we leaned into any boy's arms—we even remembered we had a mother.

Over my dead body, she said when we wanted whatever next thing it was we wanted.

Though today I come up through the basement of the house sold twenty years ago and see her and her mother in their kitchen places.

Stop it, I say to them, stop it, before I realize it was never fighting but shouting in Russian over the broil and steam.

Oh darling, my mother says, where have you been?
Was it worth it? she says when I tell her all the states I've crossed to bear myself home to her.

WOMAN WITHOUT UMBRELLA, CONFESSION

I wanted to be the one to tell you there is nothing
too small in this world to love.

Yet here I am, furious housekeeper,
stomping ants that come through

the rotting floorboards of this summer cabin.
I sweep them into the dustpan.

Toss them from the screen door. Victory.
Can you love the tidy heart of this killer?

SMOKING CIGARETTES WITH BRODSKY

I don't smoke but here I am chain smoking
with Joseph, July, 1984, Café Reggio,
one of his village spots, not the Indian haunt

where he took Nell, told her she must write
her Icarus cycle, though she wrote fiction.
Leggy, leggy, blond Virginian, it's Nell he wants

but—best friend, poet, motley diasporan—today
I'll do and do all right talking about young Musil
then Frost until he threads the conversation back to her,

Why won't she ever call me? he asks, breaks
the filter off one and then another cigarette,
while he recalls her slouch, the drape of her

sweatpants, even her refusal is adorable.
I'm 24, just back from Nicaragua on my way
to New Hampshire where, naturally, I'll make love

or revolution in a field and everything this afternoon
seems possible, has a future, the waiter bringing coffees,
MacDougal Street bangs brilliantly with trucks,

even how Joseph this minute believes it's me not Sontag
who must read the essays he's just finished.
—And have your lovely Nell call, please, okay.

I'm just learning desire makes us sometimes lovely,
always *idiotes*. And yet. And yet. And yet
Joseph smokes another cigarette.

WOMAN WITHOUT UMBRELLA, CHAPTER 3

Foxglove on the footpath. Phlox among rosemary,
roses she never sees through the bedroom window.

By late afternoon the children come home hungry,
taller, bitten—for an hour, kissable and kind,

then moody and asleep. She wants coordinates,
to run off again and find her young body waiting.

She warbles, distracted. Birds flit by the feeder.
It's empty. Here it is, a bouquet of weeds.

The chipped polish of her own floozy heart.

RESISTANCE

After the other mother and I walked that distance
to where a tidal current ran hard between sand bars,

we floated, letting the sudden water push us down,
feet swept fast from touching bottom. No one else

there in the late hour or maybe just one family,
grassy dunes behind us. Then trying to get back upstream—

no matter how hard we swam—we couldn't
make headway until we angled to the sand

and walked to the inlet's head where water
rushed us down again. And after we said

how much the kids would like it, imagining
the little one in her bright tube and the big ones

on broad backs, their large feet poking up, and after
we felt a little guilty to have this fun without kids,

then the conversation slipped to something, then
to something else and then to the next thing

one of us needed to say and we were caught
up, for an hour, in a difficult current.

UNGODLY

As if I had any power,
  was any puniest god
to choose as I did

last night in the twist
  of sleep, death
of an old school friend,

someone
  I never think about
who, last I heard, struggled,

medicated, shut in
  her house, unmarried,
no children—who'd notice?—

instead of you
  who are loved and loved
and loved.

Still I woke only mortal
  with mortal terror
that my sole power

was this imagination
  which, reckless or calculating
as all the esteemed

medicines and gods,
    would not help you
live till morning.

FLAME, SWEETHEART

The dog parades through the yard dragging maple limbs.
We envy her purpose.

Here, again, the ending. Nights, hardly. What's left to say.

Or, in a rush too much, damage fast, old damage, old grievance
we cannot bear turning from.

Your face, angular, set against me. Sulphur and mercury, a marriage.

If my love burns let the wick be.

If love is porous I will be water.
Tell me again how we found each other on a dance floor on a cul de
sac of delight.

Flame and flicker and.

Curve of the footpath up to the deck. The dog lifting her nose,
tracking scents.

Weeds that multiply in a week.

ALL THE YEARS

Our babies grown, gone from home, out where they should be
among their own, up late, chilling past any hour we'd recognize

or recognize in insomniac dread, our mornings brewed up in time
for them to head in, hooked-up with friendly benefits, as if new

terms made it new and actually different than what we took
to our creaking, narrow bed. Remember Karl. Remember Sue.

Or that fucking drummer from that fucked-up bar. Remember what
we thought it meant and sometimes did. But some nights too messed up

or with—went far past where we wanted—fast cars overturned,
speed freaks who didn't make it, a smoky tale we began to heed.

We coupled down, stayed in, stayed safe, made offspring now sprung
from home, belligerent with a hefty list of our wrongs but mostly

for our dull, sheltered, adult lives. They want to live,
to live it up. We want that too—and get through alive.

AUSPICIOUS SUBWAY

The man sitting on one side of me is reading Jean Genet and the woman on the other is reading the NY Post with the headline: Attack of the Killer Tomato. Across from me

the row of ankles are all crossed. Because, a father says to his son, Because *I* said so is why.

The doors shut then stutter open and five kids gangle in speaking Chinese. A layer of orange tulle pokes out from the hem of a blue eyelet dress.

At 42nd Street, the NY Post becomes a man in a suit holding a basket of vegetables. Two blondes ask a man in a hard hat, Should we go uptown?

A boy with a cello gets off at 68th Street and back on at 72nd where Jean Genet becomes a girl with a French textbook. Then a man with no book.

At 125th Street, a tranny with pink polished toes and delicately strapped red sandals sits down, fishes pen and paper out of her leopard bag, slips them to the man in a hardhat who writes something and hands both back to her.

At the next stop she smiles, toodleoos her purple nails before the doors close.

I get off the train at 168th, Columbia Presbyterian Hospital, and before I even show the security guard my ID he asks, How's she doing? and I say, Raring to get out of this joint. That's the right idea, he says

and I double-step five flights of stairs to the Heart ICU where I Purel
my hands, pull on mask and latex gloves, open the third curtain and
sit next to Nance on her seventh day of an induced coma, catch my
breath

and say, Just you wait, Sweetheart. Just wait till you hear what in the
world's going on out there.

MONET'S UMBRELLA

I didn't have to kneel down by the roadside lilacs
and I didn't have to go walking this dawn in Riverside

with the dog sniffing wet dirt and the red tail hawks
nesting over the Westside highway on-ramp

to know that without even trying Sweetness returns
without a Monet umbrella or a proper scarf around its neck

and that when I rush to bring Possibility indoors for a hot tea
it gathers me in for a dirty-minded kiss.

I'm ready to be every season's fool while
the bony hip of Happiness humps against my sorrow.

But where was I when rain slanted sideways
and the birds pushed into the sky?

When peonies opened, their bushy faces
bent with the burden of beauty?

When the man on the corner offered, Please,
anyone have an extra three million dollars?

And where was I when the waves folded like laundered shirts
and the grass whistled between the day's crooked thumbs?

THE WAY IT ENDED

Surprised no one. Was stunning. Had another version. Was abbreviated. Had a trap door. Was overly dramatic. Had no deus ex machina. Was riddled with cliché. Some were confused by the lack of angels.

Others felt snacks might have been served. Left a few asking questions about the tattered dress. Was the harmonica distracting? The intermission necessary? Was there a subplot? A moral? Everyone agreed the third act was a little long.

Even still, the special effects were riveting. Who could have guessed what was in the cupboard. The velvet ribbons were spectacular. The secondary characters were arguably more interesting than the protagonist. At least one person cried.

ACKNOWLEDGMENTS

I am grateful to the editors of journals and anthologies where some of these poems have appeared, though sometimes in a different form or with an entirely different title: *The Common*, *Detroit Stories*, *Dirty Words* (anthology), *Granta*, *Guernica*, *Harvard Review*, *H.O.W.*, *The Literarian*, *Massachusetts Review*, *Moonshot*, *Pequod*, *Provincetown Arts*, *The Same*, and *Washington Square*.

I am most grateful to the Atlantic Center for the Arts and Civitella Ranieri where I worked on many of these poems. My gratitude goes to friends for thoughtful readings of these poems at many stages. I am happy to have had the serious and gifted attentions of my editor Martha Rhodes. The staff of Four Way Books have my many thanks for their efforts on behalf of this book. I am grateful always to Jonah and Gabriel Redel-Traub for putting up with me. And to my husband, Bruce Van Dusen (skyline artist, word man) who keeps me laughing, curious, and then some.

"Easy Living" is for Peter Christopher.
"That's Not Even Funny" is for Jason Shinder.

Victoria Redel is the author of three books of poetry and three books of fiction. She lives in New York City and is on the faculty at Sarah Lawrence College.